Index

Projects

Basic Equipment

Rolling pin & textured pins
Rolling pin is used for rolling out the chocolate paste and covering your cakes, the textured rolling pins are used to create patterns on the paste.

Icing sugar
Used to prevent the chocolate paste from sticking to the work surface when rolling out.

Smoother
Used to guide the chocolate paste into position on your cake without touching the paste with your hands.

Plastic side scraper
Ideal for cutting off the excess paste on your cake and cake board edge, and for lifting chocolate made items without handling them.

Dusting colour
Edible Dusts that can be used to colour chocolate.

Paintbrushes
Used to paint the Dusting colours on to the chocolate.

Moulds (plastic)
Plastic moulds for setting tempered chocolate.

Moulds (silicone)
Silicone moulds for forming shapes with chocolate paste.

Sugar gun
A sugar gun is supplied with 16 different shaped attachments which can produce ropes, edible ribbon, writing or creating swirls or ribbon loops.

Frequently asked questions about chocolate paste

What is chocolate paste?

Chocolate paste is a product made from Belgian Chocolate, glucose and water. By adding glucose and water it changes the consistency of the chocolate so that it becomes pliable and therefore it can be rolled out to cover a cake, like sugarpaste, and make other edible items, for example flowers.

What is the difference between covering a cake with sugarpaste and covering it with chocolate paste?

Chocolate paste reacts to heat. As you begin to knead the paste it will soon start to become soft and possibly sticky as it interacts with your hands. It is recommended that extra icing sugar is used during the kneading and rolling out process to prevent the paste from sticking to the work surface and your hands.

What flavours are available in chocolate paste?

Tracey's Cakes chocolate paste is available in white, milk, dark, caramel, cappuccino, orange, lemon and strawberry flavours.

Will chocolate paste melt if the cake is covered in the summer months and it's a warm day?

Chocolate Paste is affected by three elements, light, heat and smell. If you place a chocolate cake in front of a window during any month of the year and the sun is directly upon it, it will melt. As a general rule, display your chocolate cake away from any direct sunlight. If it is particularly warm, try and coat your cake first thing in the morning when the humidity is lower. If you are putting a chocolate cake into a marquee in the summer consider putting the cake in just before it is required as marquees can be very humid.

Can I make chocolate roses in advance to use on a cake?

It is possible to make chocolate roses in advance, as long as they are stored in cool, dry, dark conditions.

Can I colour chocolate paste?

The best way to colour chocolate paste is to make your decorations in white chocolate paste and spray them when they are completed with PME lustre spray or dusting colours. Dusting colours are edible food colours in powder form. There are an enormous range of colours available, or you can simply create your own shades by mixing colours together. The colours are available in matt, shimmer and glittery effects. Dusting colours can be applied with a dry paintbrush, or for a more defined effect, mix a small amount of the powder with clear alcohol such as gin or vodka . Please note by adding glitter, the cake will become inedible. Only put glitter on items that are to be removed from the cake such as flowers.

Where is the best place to store my finished chocolate cake?

The best place to store your cake is in cool, dry, dark conditions. Chocolate will absorb smell so store it away from anything with a strong odour, and away from light; not only to prevent it from melting but to stop the light changing the colour of the chocolate over time. Don't be tempted to put your cake into the fridge otherwise when you take it out of the fridge it will start to condensate.

How can I make my chocolate cake shiny?

Chocolate Paste Coverings are matt finish. If you want to achieve a shiny finish or remove any excess icing sugar streaks from your cake, spray the whole cake with Edible Glaze Spray.

Preparing chocolate paste for piping

Take approx 40g of dark chocolate paste and knead it well until it is very soft and sticky. Place into a small bowl and with a palette knife dipped into **warm** water begin to soften the paste.

Repeat the procedure until the paste becomes soft enough to pass through a piping nozzle but still holds its shape, be careful not to make it too runny.

How to cover a cake & cake board with chocolate paste

You will need

Cake
Chocolate paste
Icing sugar
Buttercream
Smoother
Plastic side scraper
Sharp knife
Rolling pin
Scribing tool or sterilised pin
Cake board

To cover a cake – Step One

Before starting if the paste is very hard, place it into a microwave on full power (800W) for 10 seconds to soften it. Cut the block of paste into four smaller pieces and knead them separately. Combine the four pieces together.

To cover a cake – Step Two

Sprinkle icing sugar on to your work surface and begin to roll out your paste. Keep lifting and turning the paste a quarter turn so it doesn't stick to the work surface. Roll the paste out until it is approx 3-4 mm in thickness (1/8" – 1/6").

To cover a cake – Step Three

Carefully with the scribing tool or pin burst any air bubbles. Run your cake smoother over the paste to make sure that the paste is as even as possible.

To cover a cake – Step Four

Apply a light coating of buttercream to your cake, then carefully with a rolling pin, lift the paste on to the cake. Use the smoother to press the paste down, then slowly work down the sides of the cake with the smoother until it is all covered.

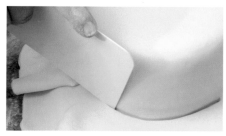

To cover a cake – Step Five

Cut off the excess paste with a plastic side scraper. Use a little icing sugar on the plastic side scraper if the paste starts to drag.

To cover the board – Step One

Paint a small amount of water on to your cake board. Roll out a strip of chocolate paste, cut a straight edge, dust the strip with a little icing sugar, then roll it up and gently guide it on to the cake board.

To cover the board – Step Two

Roll a fabric print textured rolling pin over the covered cake board to mask any joins in the paste.

To cover the board – Step Three

Cut off the excess chocolate paste using the plastic side scraper.

How to make a chocolate rose

You will need

Chocolate paste

Icing sugar

Metal petal shaped cutters

Rolling pin

Plastic side scraper

Step One

Roll out some chocolate paste onto a work surface with a light coating of icing sugar so it's not too dry then cut out 11 petals. Make a cone of chocolate paste

Step Two

Pinch the edges of each petal so they look more natural. Begin by wrapping the first petal around the cone with the point of the petal facing downwards. Make sure the centre of the cone is completely covered.

Step Three

Position the next two petals opposite each other and level with the centre of the rose, and interlink them. The paste will stick to itself; it should not need any additional sugar glue or water to stick together.

Step Four

The next row consists of three petals. Begin with the first petal and stick the left hand side down, then overlap the right hand side with the next petal, and again with the third petal. Close each petal as you go, and carefully bend the petals back to achieve a more realistic natural look. They should be positioned just about level with the centre point of the rose.

Step Five

The final row consists of five petals which are attached as described in step four. If the petals are struggling to stay in place, tip the rose upside down and use the heat of your finger to very carefully melt some of the paste encouraging the petals to stay in position.

Step Six

Use the plastic scraper to cut the rose away from the cone. Leave the rose to dry for approx an hour. This will allow the chocolate to set and hold its shape. Leave the rose matt, spray it with edible glaze to make it shiny, or colour it with lustre spray or dusting powders.

Frequently asked questions about transfer sheets

What is a transfer sheet?

A transfer sheet is an acetate sheet that has a pattern on it which is made of coloured cocoa butter. Transfer sheets are commonly associated with chocolate but recent developments mean that it is now possible to use transfer sheets on sugarpaste. Transfer sheets are for one use only; once the pattern has been removed onto the sugar or chocolate the sheet will be blank.

What patterns can I get on transfer sheets?

There are a huge number of transfer sheets available and the patterns change regularly. There are flowers, butterflies, abstract prints, animal prints, stars and swirls. Our website has over 100 designs to choose from, and they do change on a regular basis.

How do I use transfer sheets with chocolate?

Temper some Belgian Chocolate as explained on page 9 and pour on to the transfer sheet, once the chocolate has set, the pattern will be transferred. Peel off the transfer sheet to reveal the pattern. In this book there are several projects to try with chocolate and transfer sheets including cutting out panels and making individual chocolate pots.

How do I use transfer sheets with sugar paste?

Place the transfer sheet pattern side down on to rolled out sugarpaste, using a hairdryer gently heat up the transfer sheet for several minutes until the pattern has imprinted on to the sugarpaste.

Can I use transfer sheets on chocolate paste?

It is not possible to use transfer sheets directly on to chocolate paste using the same method as used to transfer them on to sugarpaste. The chocolate paste would melt with the heat of the hairdryer.

Where do I store a transfer sheet?

Transfer sheets can be stored in a cupboard, they do not require refrigeration. They can be stored flat or rolled not folded, ideally away from light to avoid any changes in colour. Transfer sheets have a use by date of up to 2 years.

How and why to dowel a cake

If you want to stack two or more cakes on top of each other, you must create an internal support system to stop the cakes from sinking into each other and potentially collapsing.

It is a straight forward procedure, involving the use of dowelling rods which are available in wood or food grade plastic from cake decorating shops; they are measured and cut to size using a knife or even secateurs.

You will need

Two cakes, usually two different sizes for example a (15cm) 6" and a (20cm) 8" cake, dowelling rods, knife or secateurs, greaseproof paper, pencil, royal icing, scissors.

TIP– The cake that is to be stacked on top of the other cake MUST have been iced on a cake board first, the same size as the cake, so the dowelling rods have something to rest against when in position.

1. Place a dowelling rod into the centre of the cake, with a pencil/pen mark where the dowel reaches the surface of the cake. Remove the dowelling rod and cut it where you have marked it. Cut 5 identical rods in length. If all the rods are equal the cake will be level, if they are different lengths the cake may tilt.

2. Push the dowels into the cake at equal distance around the cake on the base. Attach the top cake carefully, and secure with some chocolate buttercream.

What is tempering chocolate?

Tempering chocolate is the method of preparing a good quality Belgian Chocolate through heating to a controlled temperature so that it's possible to make chocolates or chocolate items that are shiny in appearance, are easy to remove from moulds and when broken they 'snap' rather than 'bend'. There are two types of chocolate available to buy; Belgian Couverture chocolate and Confectionary Chocolate. Belgian Chocolate usually contains a minimum of 32% cocoa butter and this is the best chocolate to use for decorations and has a far superior taste.

Belgian Chocolate can be easily tempered at home using a microwave, a plastic bowl, and a spatula. The bowl needs to be **plastic** as glass retains heat. There are two methods of tempering chocolate, using callets or buttons of chocolate available directly from cake decorating shops or via our website.

Microwave method – Step One

Place the chocolate into a plastic bowl, place into the microwave and heat the chocolate for 10 seconds on full power (800W). Take the chocolate out of the microwave and stir the chocolate. Place it back into the microwave and repeat the process. Do not be tempted to cheat and speed up the melting procedure otherwise the chocolate will heat up too quickly and will not temper correctly.

Microwave method – Step Two

Repeat the process until the chocolate has almost melted. Vigorously stir the chocolate to complete the melting, scraping the sides of the bowl with the plastic spatula to incorporate all of the chocolate.
Test the chocolate is ready to use by dipping in a clean palette knife into the chocolate, if it sets after 2-3 minutes the chocolate is ready to use.

Tip

If you would like to check the temperature of your chocolate, thermometers are available to purchase from cake decorating shops. Dark chocolate if correctly tempered should be 31°C (89°F) milk chocolate should be 30°C (86°F) and white chocolate should be 29°c (84°F).

Seeding method – Step One

Melt two thirds of your Belgian chocolate in the microwave in 20-30 second intervals until completely melted.

Seeding method – Step Two

Add the remaining third of the chocolate buttons to the melted chocolate and stir well until the buttons melt, bringing down the heat of the chocolate.

Dark Chocolate Lily Cake

This cake is a simple, classic chocolate cake, with all in one white chocolate paste lilies and tiny dark chocolate paste blossoms. Pipe on the extra detail with chocolate paste for a further challenge! This cake is taught in our Working with Chocolate Paste 3 class.

You will need

15cm (6") round sponge or chocolate cake on a 15cm (6") round thin cake board
25cm (10") round cake board
1kg dark chocolate paste (Tracey's Cakes)
500g white chocolate paste (Tracey''s Cakes)
Sunflower Sugar Art Lily Mould and Cutter
Flower plunger cutter

No.2 piping nozzle
Disposable piping bag
Gold ribbon (15mm in width)
Glue stick
White stamens
Dusting colours – Bright gold and chocolate (Edable Art)

Clear alcohol vodka or gin)
Buttercream – 500g
Veining tool
Turntable (optional)
Lily formers
PME edible glaze spray

Lilies – Step One

Roll out some white chocolate paste onto icing sugar. Cut out the lily shape and place it on to the veiner, push the veiner together to mark both sides of the paste.

Lilies – Step Two

Paint the edge of the lily with a damp paintbrush (water) and use the veining tool to seal the lily by rolling it gently back and forth across the join. Leave the lily to dry on the form for at least a couple of hours.

Lilies – Step Three

Dust the centre of the lily petals with the chocolate dusting powder. Mix a small amount of the powder with alcohol and paint dots on to the lily. Push a tiny ball of dark chocolate paste into the centre of the lily, cut the stamens and insert them into the paste.

To Complete The Cake – Step One

Dampen the cake board with water, cover the board with chocolate paste. Coat the cake as per instructions on page 6. Attach the ribbon to the base of the cake with a little piece of chocolate paste. Prepare some chocolate paste for piping as shown on page 5, pipe the dots evenly around the cake. Begin with the first line above the ribbon. After ten dots, take a damp paintbrush and make sure the peaks of the dots are pushed down.

To Complete The Cake – Step Two

Roll out the chocolate paste onto icing sugar so it's quite thin. Press the plunger flower cutters into the paste in assorted sizes. On the back of each flower roll a tiny ball of dark chocolate paste, press the plunger cutter onto the cake or board and the flower petals will stand upright.

To Complete The Cake – Step Three

Roll a tiny ball of dark chocolate paste into Bright Gold dusting powder. Brush a tiny amount of clear alcohol into the centre of each flower and place the gold ball. Attach the lilies to the cake with some softened dark chocolate paste. Spray the whole cake with Edible glaze spray to create a shiny effect.

Pink heart cake

This double height cake is easier to cover than it looks! Cutting strips of chocolate paste and laying them on one by one, means it's easy to create a two tone effect. Experiment with textured rolling pins to get different patterns on the panels.

You will need

(35cm) 14" drum
2 x (15cm) 6" round thin cake boards
(23cm) 9" round thin cake board
4 x (15cm) 6" round sponge or chocolate cakes (each cake (5cm) 2" in height (total (20cm) 8" height)
4 x (23cm) 9" round sponge or chocolate cakes (each cake (5cm) 2" in height (total (20cm) 8" height)
Chocolate buttercream
1kg strawberry flavoured chocolate paste
800g white chocolate paste
500g white chocolate
Blossom Sugar Art Hydrangea Cutter
Jem Daisy textured rolling pin
Gold ribbon 15mm wide – 1.5 metres
Gold sheer ribbon – 40mm wide – 8 metres
4 flower picks
FMM Multi ribbon cutter
8 x gold 24g wire
Large chocolate heart mould (Life of the party 08886)

Step One

Paint the cake drum with water, roll out some strawberry chocolate paste onto some icing sugar. Place the paste onto the board, then roll the daisy rolling pin across the paste to mark it. Cut off the excess paste.

Step Two

Place two (23cm) 9" cakes on 9" board and the other two on to the 14"round drum. Dowel the cakes using the method shown on page 8. Repeat for the 6" cakes on the same board size, then place the four 6" cakes on the 9" cakes.

Step Three

Roll out white chocolate paste and strawberry chocolate paste, cut strips of paste 2" (5cm) wide x height of the cake plus some extra to cover the top of the cake. Roll the textured daisy rolling pin across the strawberry paste. Secure each strip to the cake with some white chocolate buttercream.

Step Four

Make twelve gold ribbon loops, by folding two loops of ribbon together and securing them with some wire tied around the bottom of the loops.

Step Five

Melt some white chocolate as described on page 9 and pour into the heart chocolate mould. Place into the fridge and leave to set completely for approx 20 minutes. Make some large strawberry roses as described on page 7.

Step Six

Roll out white chocolate paste onto icing sugar, and cut out some hydrangeas using the metal cutter. Place them on to the double sided silicone veiner and press it down. Leave to dry for a couple of hours.

Step Seven

Use some softened white chocolate paste behind the large chocolate hearts to prop them up and secure them to the cake. Push the end of the ribbon loops into flower picks behind the hearts. Do not push wire directly into the cake. Add the hydrangeas and roses. Spray the whole cake with edible glaze .

Rock and roll guitar cake

This cake is perfect for those who love music! If you prefer a lighter shade, switch your chocolate to milk or white chocolate, the design is as flexible as you need it to be. Even use a different mould for different instruments!

You will need

20cm (6") and 25cm (8") square chocolate or sponge cakes
850g dark chocolate buttercream
(20cm) 6" square thin cake board
(29cm) 11" square drum
500g dark belgian chocolate
250g dark chocolate paste (Tracey's Cakes)

1 music transfer sheet
Guitar mould
Approx 70 dark chocolate cigarellos (10cm long)
600g dark chocolate curls
PME edible glaze spray
Star cutter (any size)
Bright gold dust (Edable Art)

Clear alcohol eg. gin, vodka
1 wooden skewer
5 dowels
Secateurs
Ruler
Glue stick
Gold ribbon (15mm wide)

To make the guitars - Step One

Polish the guitar moulds with a piece of cotton wool to make the mould clean and shiny.

To make the guitars - Step Two

Temper 150g of the dark chocolate as described on page 9 and pour into the guitar mould. Tap the mould onto the work surface to ensure any air bubbles in the chocolate rise to the surface. Place in the fridge for 20 minutes.

To make the music panels

Spread some tempered chocolate onto the transfer sheet, approx 2-3 mm thick and wait 1-2 minutes for the chocolate to start to set. When the chocolate has started to look 'dull' in appearance cut out the panels measuring 10cm x 4cm. Place the transfer sheet in the fridge and leave to dry for approx 20 minutes.

To complete the cake - Step One

Place the 8" cake onto the 11" drum in the centre, and the 6" cake on to the 6" thin board. Dowel the cakes as per instructions on page 8. Coat the two cakes in a layer of chocolate buttercream and place the pre-made panels onto the cake then 3-4 cigarellos, then another panel.

To complete the cake - Step Two

Secure the chocolate guitars to the cake using a little chocolate buttercream. Attach the long skewer with a little chocolate buttercream on to the back of one of the guitars on the top of the cake, so that it supports the guitar standing up.

To complete the cake - Step Three

Cut out some star shapes from dark chocolate paste and paint them with bright gold dust mixed with clear alcohol. Stick them on to the cake with a little buttercream. Attach the gold ribbon to the edge of the board with a glue stick.

Teddy bear cake

A very simple cake idea for beginners and perfect for lots of occasions, including birthdays and christenings. This cake can easily be adapted to any colour, by changing the dusting colour of the panel behind the bear. Have fun and try some different shades.

You will need

15cm (6") round sponge cake or chocolate cake	Sugargun	FMM multi ribbon cutter
23cm (9") round cake drum	Pale blue and black dusting powder	Glue stick
750g caramel flavoured chocolate paste (Tracey's Cakes)	Round cutter, 7cm diameter (3")	Clear alcohol (vodka or gin)
Buttercream	Cocktail stick	Sugar glue
250g white chocolate paste (Tracey's Cakes)	Brown ribbon 15mm	Teddy mould

Step One

Paint the cake drum with water, roll out some dark chocolate paste and cover the cake board. Cover the cake with the caramel flavoured chocolate paste as shown on page 6. Roll out some white chocolate paste onto some icing sugar. Roll your textured rolling pin across the paste.

Step Two

Cut out a circle of white paste and with a large paintbrush carefully dust the plaque blue or any colour of your choice.

Step Three

Paint a small area on the middle of the cake with sugar glue and place the dusted plaque into position. Take another piece of paste, roll it in icing sugar and then push it into the teddy mould. Bend the mould back slightly to release the bear.

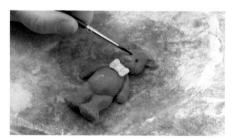

Step Four

Paint the features on the bear with a little black food colouring mixed with a small amount of clear alcohol. Make a little bow from the mould with white chocolate paste and dust it blue to match the plaque. Secure the bear to the plaque with a little sugar glue.

Step Five

Cut out a strip of white chocolate paste, that has been textured using the FMM multi ribbon cutter 3.5cm wide, dust it with blue, then attach to the base of the cake using a little sugar glue. Using the half moon attachment for a sugar gun, place some white chocolate paste into the barrel of the gun, and push some paste through it.

Step Six

Brush the strip of white chocolate paste with blue, then gently with a cocktail stick, mark the paste at even intervals. Attach to the edge of the cake and around the plaque with a little sugar glue. Secure the brown ribbon to the cake board edge with a glue stick.

Disco purple roses cake

A modern brightly coloured chocolate cake, double height with high impact disco purple coloured roses reflecting against the dark chocolate.
For a more subtle finish, try covering the cake in white chocolate and dusting or spraying the roses a different colour.

You will need

Two 15cm (6") round cakes (3" in height each)
15cm (6") round thin cake board
25cm (10") round cake drum
Plastic dowels
Buttercream
1.5kg dark chocolate paste (Tracey's Cakes)

250g white chocolate paste (Tracey's Cakes)
FMM multi ribbon cutter
Blossom Sugar Art Petunia Cutter
African violet and black, dusting powder
(Edable Art) Disco Purple (Edable Art)
non toxic, *not to be consumed*

Large metal rose petal cutter
PME glaze spray
1.5 metres of 15mm brown ribbon
Glue stick
Butterfly lace mould

To make butterflies – Step One
Take a small piece of dark chocolate paste and roll it in some icing sugar. Push the paste carefully and quickly into the mould. Bend the silicone mould back and release the butterfly.

To make butterflies – Step Two
Leave the butterflies to dry on a piece of folded paper for approx 2-3 hours.

To make roses
Follow the instructions on page 7. To make your roses, you will need three full blown roses, four mid blown roses and two buds. Spray the roses with Edible Glaze then sprinkle some glitter on to the roses. The spray will make the glitter stick to the flowers.

To make blossoms
Follow the instructions on page 28. To make the blossoms, carefully dust them with African violet dust and paint the detail with black
dusting powder mixed with a little clear alcohol.

To decorate the cake – Step One
Cover the cake board. Place one cake on to the cake drum and the other on to the thin cake board. Dowel the bottom cake as explained on page 9. Place the second cake on top and coat the whole cake in chocolate buttercream. Roll out the dark chocolate paste approx 2-3mm thick. Set the FMM ribbon cutter to 4cm (1 ½" wide) and cut a strip 15cm (6") in height. Secure the strip to the cake with chocolate buttercream.

To decorate the cake – Step Two
Stick the flowers and the butterflies to the cake with some softened pieces of chocolate paste, spray the whole cake with the glaze spray. Attach the 15mm wide brown ribbon to the cake board edge with a glue stick. Keep the glitter on the top petals of the rose, to avoid any glitter coming in to contact with the surface of the cake. The glitter roses are for decoration only and should not be consumed.

Chocolate bunting cake

A vintage-inspired bunting cake with soft shades of green (lemon flavoured chocolate paste) and pink (strawberry flavoured chocolate paste) flags.
A perfect wedding cake for a summer's day.

You will need

- 10cm (4"), 15cm (6") and 20cm (8") round sponge or chocolate cakes
- 10cm (4") and 15cm (6") thin round cake boards
- 28cm (11") round drum
- 1kg (2lb 3oz) white belgian chocolate
- 3kg (6½lb) white chocolate paste (Tracey's Cakes)
- Buttercream
- 250g lemon flavoured chocolate paste (Tracey's Cakes)

- 500g strawberry flavoured chocolate paste (Tracey's Cakes)
- 100g milk chocolate paste (Tracey's Cakes)
- Nine plastic dowels
- Square cutter 4cm (1½")
- Sugargun
- PME nozzle number 4
- Orchard Vari Pin
- Jem Flower rolling pin

- Royal icing in a disposable piping bag
- Teardrop shaped metal cutter 2½cm (1") at the widest point
- Double-sided silicone leaf veiner
- 1.5m brown 15mm wide ribbon
- Glue stick
- Sugar glue

Step One

Place the two smaller cakes on to the same size cake boards, then 8" cake on the 11" cake drum in the middle. Cover the cake and board as shown on page 6 with white chocolate paste. Dowel and stack the cakes as shown on page 9. Create a border using the sugar gun as described on page 17.

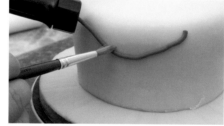

Step Two

Change the attachment on the sugar gun to the larger of the two round holes. Place milk chocolate paste into the sugar gun, and gently squeeze out the paste to form a long string which the bunting will hang from. Carefully stick the paste to the cake with either sugar glue or a little royal icing.

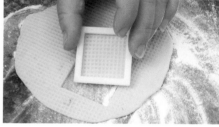

Step Three

Roll out the lemon and strawberry chocolate paste to approx 2mm thickness. Texture the strawberry paste, with the Jem Flower rolling pin. Cut out some squares using the square cutter, then cut them in half to form triangles. On the lemon Flavoured paste use another textured rolling pin and cut out squares.

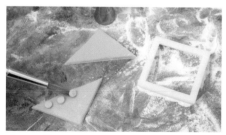

Step Four

Roll out 100g of the strawberry paste, cut out some squares, and cut these in half. Roll out some lemon flower paste as thinly as possible. Using a number 4 nozzle cut out some tiny circles of chocolate paste and carefully with a damp paintbrush (water or sugar glue) place the dots into rows on to the plain pink bunting.

Step Five

Attach the flags to the cake with some royal icing. To make the leaves, roll out some lemon paste to approx 3mm thick and cut out 8 leaves with the teardrop shaped cutter. Place the leaves onto the double-sided veiner and gently press it to make the pattern.

Step Six

Pinch the back of the leaves so they don't dry flat, attach them to the cake with a little royal icing. Attach the medium size roses (instructions to make the roses can be found on page 7). Using a glue stick attach the brown ribbon to the edge of the cake board.

Individual daisy pots

A taste of spring with these cute little daisy chocolate cake boxes; present one in a clear box for a perfect gift for Mother's Day or a birthday. These cakes are created in our 'Working witth Chocolate Part 3' class.

You will need

(15cm) 6" square sponge cake or chocolate cake
White chocolate buttercream
1 green lines transfer sheet (Tracey's Cakes)
500g white belgian chocolate
500g white chocolate paste (Tracey's Cakes)
300g white chocolate curls

Sugarglue
Metal cutter measuring 5cm x 5cm (2" x 2")
Yellow and green dusting powder
PME Sunflower/Daisy cutter 45mm
Sharp knife
Gem Daisy centre mould

To make the daisies - Step One

Roll out some white chocolate paste on to some icing sugar to approx 1.5mm (¹⁄₆th") thick. Cut out two small flowers with the Daisy Cutter.

To make the daisies - Step Two

To make the centre of the daisy, roll a small ball of paste in some icing sugar then gently press into the Gem Flower centre mould. Dust the centre of the daisy with some yellow dusting colour before assembling the flower.

To make the daisies - Step Three

Lay the first flower onto the plastic former, paint a small amount of sugarglue into the middle and add the second flower so the petals overlap each other, finally add the centre of the flower with a little sugarglue.

To make the daisies - Step Four

Dust around the centre of the flower lightly with a little green dusting powder. Leave to set at room temperature overnight.

To make the cake - Step One

Cut out squares of sponge cake measuring 5cm x 5cm (2" x 2") with a sharp knife or a metal cutter. Coat each cake with a thin layer of buttercream, then cover them individually with white chocolate paste.

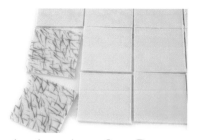

To make the cake - Step Two

Melt the chocolate as described on page 9 and pour on to the transfer sheets as described on page 32. Wait 2-3 minutes for the chocolate to start to dry, then using a sharp knife cut squares of chocolate measuring 5.5cm x 5.5cm (2 ¼"). Leave to dry for approx 20-30mins.

To make the cake - Step Three

Peel the transfer sheet off the chocolate, and with a little white chocolate buttercream, stick the four panels together to form a box. Sprinkle in the white chocolate curls to the top, add the daisy and secure in place with a little buttercream.

Pink heart cigarello cake

A touch of luxury with white chocolate and raspberries.
Fill your cake with a double layer of milk chocolate buttercream and serve with some additional red fruit and ice cream.

You will need

25cm (8") heart shaped cake, sponge or chocolate cake	300g dark chocolate curls
28cm (11") cake drum	1.25 metres of 40mm wide pink ribbon
White chocolate buttercream	1 metre of 15mm wide pink sparkly ribbon
90 white cigarellos	Pink silk butterfly
Edable Art – Iced Pink dusting powder	PME glaze spray
Small punnet of raspberries (150g)	Glue stick

Tip

Store the cake at room temperature, not in the fridge and away from direct sunlight.

Step One

Coat the sides of your cake with buttercream. Dust one side of the white cigarellos with the iced pink dusting powder, away from the cake so the excess dusting powder is on the work surface not the cake.

Step Two

Carefully stick the cigarellos on to the cake, so that the pink side of the cigarello is facing the outside edge of the cake.

Step Three

Coat the top of the cake on the cake with white chocolate buttercream, then place raspberries all around the edge of the heart cake.

Step Four

Sprinkle some dark chocolate curls on to the remaining surface of the cake and cake board.

Step Five

To make the dark chocolate curls shiny, spray them with some glaze spray.

Step Six

Position the butterfly in place with some buttercream and tie a bow around the cake to complete the design.

Candy cake

The ultimate sweet shop on a cake! Brightly coloured lollies and poured chocolate over a white chocolate cake. Look out for the chocolate rabbits hiding behind the chocolate flowers!

You will need

- 10cm (4"), 15cm (6") & 20cm (8") round sponge or chocolate cakes
- 10cm (4") and 15cm (6") thin round cake boards
- 28cm (11") round drum
- 1kg (2lb 3oz) white chocolate
- 3kg (6½lb) white chocolate paste (Tracey's Cakes)
- White chocolate buttercream
- 500g milk chocolate buttons

- Sugar glue
- 400g white chocolate buttons
- 75g strawberry flavoured buttons
- 25g lemon flavoured buttons
- Chocolate coloured sweets
- Rabbit mould
- Flower mould
- Heart mould

- Lollipop sticks
- Transfer sheet candy stripes (Tracey's Cakes)
- Sugar gun
- 1.5 metres 15mm wide brown ribbon
- Glue stick
- Disposable piping bag

Candy striped lollies - Step One
Temper the white chocolate using the instructions on page 9. Place the chocolate into a piping bag, cut off the end and squeeze the chocolate onto a transfer sheet. Keep the piping bag in the middle of the lolly stop squeezing when you are happy with the size of the lolly.

Candy striped lollies - Step Two
Roll a lollipop stick into the chocolate and leave to dry for approx 20-30mins either at room temperature or in the fridge.

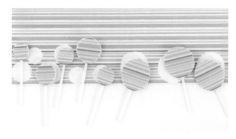

Candy striped lollies - Step Three
Remove the lollipops, by carefully lifting them off the transfer sheet and the pattern will have imprinted on to the chocolate.

Flowers, rabbits & heart
Temper the relevant colour chocolate using the instructions on page 9. Place the chocolate into a piping bag and pipe the chocolate into the mould, until it is three quarters full. Tap the mould on the work surface to bring the air bubbles to the surface and place in the fridge to set for 30 mins.

To complete the cake - Step One
Place the two smaller cakes on to the same size cake board and the 8" cake on the 11" cake drum. Cover the cakes and board as shown on page 6 with white chocolate paste. Dowel the cakes as shown on page 8. Using the sugar gun with the half moon attachment create a border of with white chocolate paste, stick the paste to the cake with a little sugar glue.

To complete the cake - Step Two
Temper the chocolate as per instructions on page 9 carefully and slowly pour the milk chocolate over the cake allowing it to run freely. Whilst it is starting to set, carefully stick on some of the chocolate items and sweets etc. Attach the brown ribbon to the edge of the cake board with a glue stick.

Chocolate blossom cupcakes

Quick and easy chocolate cupcakes, using an all in one cutter and veiner; incredibly effective and simple to make with stunning results.

You will need

12 chocolate cupcakes	Red and black dusting powder
(receipe for chocolate cake on page 34)	Large plastic star nozzle
Chocolate buttercream	Disposable piping bag
Blossom sugar art	250g white chocolate paste (Tracey's Cakes)
Petunia cutter	Clear alcohol (vodka or gin)

To make the blossoms – Step One

Roll out some white chocolate paste onto some icing sugar approx 2mm in thickness.

To make the blossoms – Step Two

Using the metal cutter cut out a flower, place it on to the veiner.

To make the blossoms – Step Three

Press the veiner together, open the veiner and bend the silicone mould back slightly so the flower is released, leave to dry for a couple of hours at room temperature.

To make the blossoms – Step Four

Dust the flower with red dusting powder, mix a little black dusting powder with some clear alcohol and paint some dots on to the flower.

To pipe the cupcake – Step One

Fill the piping bag with chocolate buttercream, hold the piping bag vertically over the cupcake edge with the nozzle held just slightly above the surface of the cake. Squeeze the bag gently and as the chocolate buttercream starts to come through the nozzle move the bag in an anti clockwise direction towards the centre of the cake.

To pipe the cupcake – Step Two

At the middle of the cupcake, stop squeezing the bag and lift the nozzle away. Place the blossom onto the cake whilst the buttercream is still sticky.

Pink leopard print handbag

Transform any bag with transfer sheets, with over 100 to choose from, our basic bag structure can be recreated in many different patterns, from leopard print to tartan.

You will need

3 x (23cm) 9" x (15cm) 6" sponge cake
(30cm) 12" round board
1kg buttercream
Palette knife
Sharp knife for carving cake
2 x leopard print transfer sheets (Tracey's Cakes)
Hairdryer

2kg cerise pink sugarpaste
500g black sugar paste
250g cerise pink flower paste (A Piece of Cake)
Stitching wheel
FMM multi ribbon cutter
Sugar glue
Ribbon

Glue stick
Greaseproof paper
Pencil
Orchard Products all in one rose cutter
Small circle metal cutter

In advance – Step One

Roll out the flower paste on icing sugar, until approx 2-3mm thick using the FMM multi ribbon cutter, cut out two strips to form the handles of the handbag. Lay the strips across either two rolling pins or two cardboard tubes and leave to dry for 24 hours.

Step Two

Place the first of the 3 cakes onto the 12" round board, secure with buttercream. Fill the cakes with buttercream and place all three cakes together. Trim the cakes to form the shape of the handbag. Cut out two templates, one for the front and back of the cake and one for the top and side using greaseproof paper.

Step Three

Roll out the pink sugarpaste onto icing sugar. Place the front template onto the sugarpaste and cut around it with a knife. Place the transfer sheet printed side down on to the sugarpaste. Hold the transfer sheet down with the smoother and switch on the hairdryer. Working in a steady circular motion, heat the transfer sheet for approx 2 minutes.

Step Four

Check on the process of the transfer by carefully peeling back a small corner to see if the pattern is transferring, if not continue to heat for a further minute. Peel off the transfer sheet and place the section of sugar paste onto the cake, trim to fit with a knife, repeat the process for the back and top of the cake.

Step Five

Using the cutting wheel cut out thin strips of pink sugarpaste to cover the joins on the bags. Adjust the cutting wheel size and cut out wider pieces of sugarpaste to form the straps of the bag and detail, see pic above. Attach to the cake using sugar glue. Use the stitching wheel to add further detail to your cake particularly on the straps.

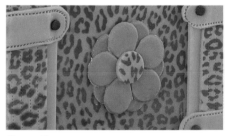

Step Six

Cover the cake board using the instructions on page 6 with black sugarpaste. Carefully push the handles of the bag into the top of the cake. Cut out a flower from the plain pink flower paste, and a small circle from the leopard print sugarpaste, and attach to the cake with sugar glue to complete your design.

Transfer sheet pots

The endless options to these lovely little chocolate pots are only restricted by your imagination. Look carefully at the transfer sheet you choose before deciding which chocolate to try; the difference in the look can be quite spectacular!

You will need

Small cake – 5cm (2") diameter x 4cm (1½") height
Buttercream
Chocolate paste
Transfer sheets

Belgian chocolate
Decoration
Tape measure
Large pallette knife

Step One

Cover your small cake with a thin layer of buttercream, then roll out some chocolate paste and cover your little cake using the method described on page 6.

Step Two

Measure the circumference of your cake and add 1.5cm (½") to the measurement so that the transfer sheet will overlap. The transfer sheet should be 5cm (2") in height, just so that it is a little bit taller than the cake. Cut out the transfer sheet strip carefully.

Step Three

Temper some chocolate using the instructions on page 9. Place the transfer sheet strip on to the work surface with the pattern side facing towards you and carefully, with a palette knife, spread the chocolate across the sheet so that the transfer sheet is completely covered and unable to see the pattern (approx 2mm (1/8") thick).

Step Four

As soon as you have spread the chocolate, pick up the transfer sheet on the edges of the strip, *not the top*. Wrap the sheet around the cake towards you.

Step Five

Stick one side of the sheet to the cake then wrap the rest of it around the cake overlapping the sheets at the end. Leave to dry, preferably in a fridge for 20 minutes.

Step Six

Peel the transfer sheet away carefully to reveal the pattern. At the point of overlap continue to pull the transfer sheet and it will gently snap the chocolate to create a straight line join.

Design ideas

There are so many ways to decorate the transfer sheet pots, here are a few ideas to try. These mini cakes are made on our Working with Chocolate Paste Part 2 class.

Think carefully about the colour of the pattern of the transfer sheet before commencing, as this can dictate which type of chocolate is possible to use. For example, a leopard print pattern which is dark would be difficult to see on dark chocolate, and possibly milk, so white chocolate or a coloured chocolate like orange would be recommended as shown here.

A white pattern such as musical notes would be faint and difficult to see on white chocolate but on dark chocolate the contrast is dramatic, shown here with the guitar mini cake.

Some transfer sheets can change in appearance depending on which chocolate is used. For example the basket weave pattern shown here is pink in appearance when used with dark chocolate by contrast appears blue when used with white chocolate

Experiment with different colour chocolate, and toppers; lollipops make great focal points for these little cakes.

Present your finished item in a clear box, they are a perfect size for a personalised gift, such as a thank you, teachers present or for mothers day.

Recipes

Chocolate cake

1. Preheat the oven to 165°C (325°F/ Gas 3). Grease your cake tin, and line with greaseproof paper.

2. Beat the butter and margarine together, add one egg at a time with a tablespoon of flour per egg, mix well. Add the milk.

3. Finally add the remaining flour and cocoa powder, and carefully incorporate them into the mixture.

4. Place the mixture into your tin and bake in the middle of the oven. To see if the cake is cooked, place a skewer into the centre of the cake. If it comes out clean then the cake is ready.

5. Leave the cake in its tin to stand for 5 minutes before attempting to remove it and cool on a wire rack.

For cupcakes, cook for 35 minutes at same temperature.

Chocolate buttercream

125g Soft butter
375g Icing sugar
Tablespoon of water
125g melted chocolate

1. Beat the butter, icing sugar and water together with ideally a food mixer until pale in colour.

2. Add the melted chocolate and continue to beat it. If the mixture starts to become stiff add more water. Buttercream without chocolate added to it will keep in the fridge for up to 3 weeks. Try to avoid storing buttercream in the fridge that contains chocolate as the cold temperature will make it set very hard and it willthen be difficult to use. Add the chocolate when you require it.

Ganache

180ml (6floz) heavy cream
200g (7oz) dark chocolate buttons
25g (1oz) butter

1. Heat the cream and the butter and pour over the dark chocolate buttons

2. Stir the mixture until it is smooth.

The basic mixture can be enhanced with the addition of alcohol or flavouring extracts.

Ganache will keep once made in the fridge in an air tight container for approx 2 weeks. The addition of any alcohol will extend the shelf life to 4 weeks.

Sugar glue

Used for attaching some items to the cakes.

30ml of water with approx a quarter of a teaspoon of CMC or Tylose Powder

Mix two together and store in a small pot. It can be purchased pre-made from sugarcraft shops.

Royal icing

Royal icing
2-3 Large Eggs
450g Icing Sugar
(make sure your bowl is completely clean and grease-free before you start)

1. Beat the egg whites only with a hand held whisk until they are frothy.

2. Add the sieved icing sugar a little at a time and keep beating the mixture until all the icing sugar is completely incorporated.

Do not store in the fridge. Store at room temperature in an airtight plastic container.

Chocolate Cake or Cupcakes

Square tin		15cm (6")	18cm (7")	20cm (8")	25cm (10")
Round tin	15cm (6")	18cm (7")	20cm (8")	23cm (9")	
Soft Butter	120g	175g	225g	290g	450g
Caster Sugar	120g	175g	225g	290g	450g
Eggs	2	3	4	5	9
Self raising flour	100g	150g	185g	245g	400g
Cocoa powder	25g	30g	35g	40g	45g
Milk	15ml (1tbsp)	30ml (2tbsp)	30ml (2tbsp)	45ml (3tbsp)	60ml (4tbsp)
Cooking time	1 ¼ hours	1 ¼ hours	1 ¾ hours	2 hours	2 ¼ hours